# WHO AM I?

I am green and croaky, smooth and slimy.
I live in ponds and lakes.

# WHO AM I?

By Moira Butterfield
Illustrated by Wayne Ford

Belitha Press

First published in the UK in 1997 by
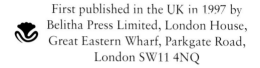
Belitha Press Limited, London House,
Great Eastern Wharf, Parkgate Road,
London SW11 4NQ

ISBN 1 85561 700 5 (hardback)
ISBN 1 85561 756 0 (paperback)

British Library Cataloguing in Publication Data for this book
is available from the British Library.

Printed in Hong Kong

Editor: Stephanie Bellwood
Designer: Helen James
Illustrator: Wayne Ford / Wildlife Art Agency
Consultant: Andrew Branson

My skin is wet.
My legs are strong.
They help me hop and swim along.
To catch a meal
I leap up high
and wrap my tongue around a fly.

Who am I?

# Here is my eye

I hide in the weeds in the pond where I live. Only my eyes stick up above the water.

Can you spot my ears? They are the big circles behind my eyes.

# Here are my back legs

When an insect
flies over my head
I push on my strong
back legs and leap
out of the water.

I move so fast
through the air
that this tasty moth
won't see me coming.

# Here is my tongue

It shoots out of my mouth and wraps around the moth. Then it disappears back into my mouth.

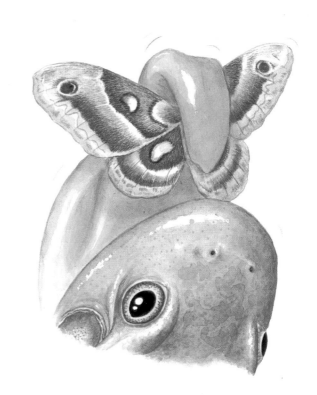

I like to eat all kinds of small animals. I might even try to catch a duckling.

# Here are my back feet

They are webbed.
This means that there
is skin stretched
between each toe.
It helps me to swim.

My feet help me
to hop. I look out
for big animals who
want to eat me, like
that hungry heron.

# Here are my front legs

I have four long
thin front toes.
I use them to
push food into
my wide mouth.

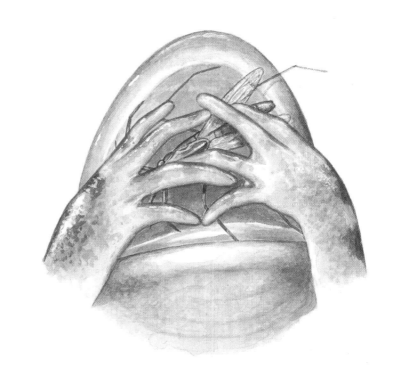

I like to sit down and
rest on my front legs.
I sit in the long grass
and look for food.

# Here is my skin

My skin is smooth
and very slimy.
It is green, grey
and yellow.
I can hide in the
green pond weed.

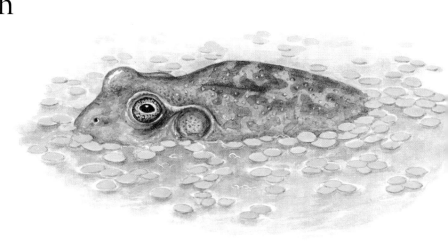

When I am underwater
I breathe through my skin.
When I am on land
I breathe through
my nose like you.

# Here is my throat

Sometimes I call to other animals like me.
I blow my throat out like a balloon and
make a deep groaning noise.

You can hear me a long way away ...
# croak!
Have you guessed who I am?

# I am a frog

Point to my…

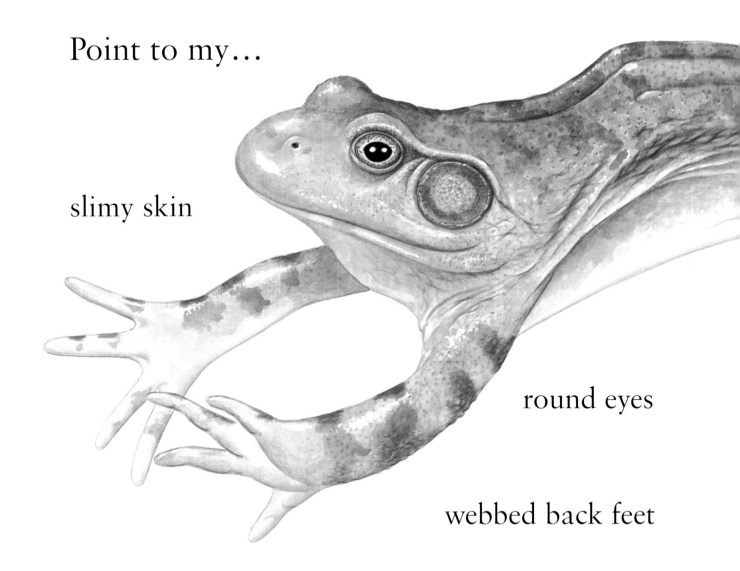

slimy skin

round eyes

webbed back feet

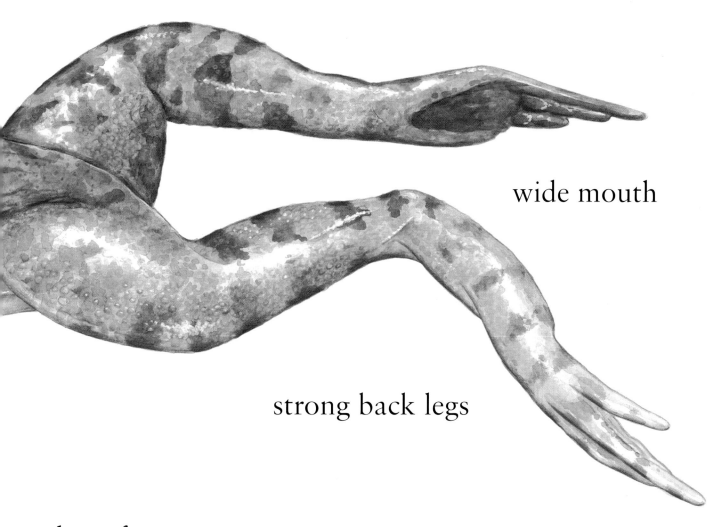

wide mouth

strong back legs

long front toes

I am called an
American bullfrog.

# Here is a baby bullfrog

It starts as a tiny egg
in a lump of eggs
called frogspawn.
A tadpole hatches
out of the egg.

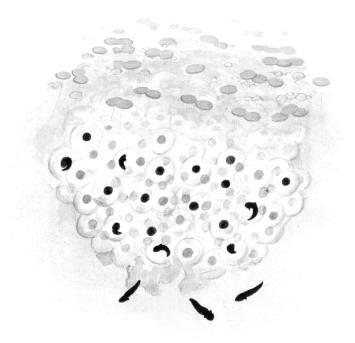

The tadpole looks
like a little fish.
Then it starts to
grow legs. Slowly
it turns into a frog.

# Here is my home

I live in ponds, lakes and swamps.

How many bullfrogs can you find?
Can you see two spotted turtles,
a pond-skater and a water snake?

# Here is a map of the world

I live in
North America.
Where is it
on the map?

North
America

Can you point to the
place where you live?

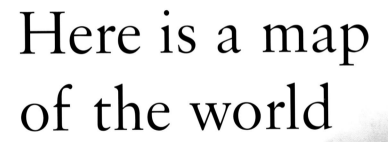

# Can you answer these questions about me?

What does my skin feel like?

Why are my webbed back feet useful?

What do I like to eat?

What are baby frogs called?

What do my
ears look like?

How do I catch
my food?

What do I use
my front legs for?

Where do I live?

What colour is my skin?

# Here are some words to learn about me

**breathe** To take air in and let it out of my body. This keeps me alive. I can breathe through my nose or my skin.

**frogspawn** A lump of frog's eggs floating in water. The eggs turn into tadpoles.

**leap** To make a big high jump.

**slimy** Something that feels wet and slippery.

**tadpole** The name for a baby frog. A tadpole grows slowly into a frog.

**throat** The back of my mouth. I blow out my throat and make a loud noise.

**swamp** A watery muddy place.

**webbed** A webbed foot has skin stretched between each toe. My back feet are webbed.

**weeds** Wild plants that grow fast. I like to hide in the green pond weed.